ACING
THE IMPOSSIBLE

Faith in the Other Dimension

CHARLES MWEWA

To those who may encounter situations that are beyond the realm of nature and human effort to overcome.

CONTENTS

When I saw a little child, I was almost given up for death. But I survived, I lived. Although I can barely remember the event, I have some synoptic memories of me being in intensive care unit surrounded by tubes. But I knew I was safe, even when my mother sat there crying and worried. At another time, during my illness, my parents would find me out of bed, on the bedroom floor, even when I had no strength to move. I believe in the miraculous. I believe in impossibilities.

To be safe in life, it is better to have both reason and faith on your side. It does not do good to only major in one at the expense of the other. Reason and science are our best friends; and so is faith in God.

In this little treatise, I show you how to extend your level of faith from the reasonable realm into the "other" realm, the place where impossible becomes possible.

c.m.

IMPOSSIBILITIES TO POSSIBILITIES

Between June and August 2023, I was trying to force my mind to conceive what are called impossibilities. It's been a raw deal and a real run. At any rate, I found myself stretching my brain further and further until it gave up. Then I realized that there was another way led for us.

So, what started all this?

The Bible, you guessed right. There is a scriptural verse in the Bible, usually overlooked or just used for its beautiful sound, that, I believe is the key to unlocking the impossible.

It is the following lines: "Now unto him that is able to do exceedingly, abundantly above all that we ask or think, according to the power that worketh in us, unto him be glory in the church by Christ Jesus throughout all ages, world without end. Amen."[1]

Apostle Paul's prayer for Europe, to the Turkeys, the Ephesians, can unlock more than just blessings, but a whole lot of other things. It is a revelatory prayer, not just about who God is and what He can do, but of the existence of other dimensions undeciphered by the human minds.

In that other dimension, what we call impossible, is the daily reality called the possible. Here are four things that Paul is trying to share.

First, that God can: "God is able." The other day, I was at a prayer meeting and a beloved sister-in-Christ attended to receive prayers against the cancer from which she was suffering.

---

[1] Ephesians 3:20-21

She came because she had faith.

Her family who accompanied her were struggling to keep their own faith strong. I was asked to pray for her. As I began to pray, I relied upon, among other verses, the above scripture.

That God can.

This is because, humanly speaking, cancer seems like an impossibility. We know that because the miracle of medical science has failed to find its cure. So, to pray against cancer successfully, we ought to visit another realm – a dimension where God is – because He is not limited by the impossible.

In fact, Paul once wrote of "the God who gives life to the dead and calls into being things that were not."[2]

God gives life to dead things.

That means that even death, in the sight of God, is not an impossibility. And that is our faith and hope in the resurrection of the dead,

---

[2] Romans 4:17

isn't it? Because we believe that death does not end our existence; God will resurrect us at the Last Day.

But we see another dimension here, that God calls things that we the humans call impossibilities, possible. He calls, as it were, "things that are not as if they were."

Second, the human mind is limited: "above all that we ask or think." Other translations render "think," as imagine or imagination. In short, we do not have a human facility that can out-think the impossible.

We are limited.

Thinking the impossible is beyond our current mental framework.

When I was a student in boarding school, I had firsthand experience of this verse of scripture. I needed transport money to travel back home after the schools closed.

I had no money.

So, I prayed.

I waited.

The very last day before the boarding would evacuate everyone from its hostels, the money came. God was not too early, He wasn't too late, either.

God was on time.

Now, I have a habit, I don't flinch when I pray, God always answers me in real time. It's a glorious habit.

Praise be to His name.

To receive results from our walk with God and our prayers, we must shift our thinking into the faith mode – the "other" dimension – and then stop trusting our own human imagination and start to trust the "other" imaginations into the impossible.

Once we add human reasoning to our prayers, we drown our chances of receiving miracles and the impossible. When we give reasonable explanations for why God should or should not answer our prayers, we injure our likelihood to receiving from God. If we pray for money, for example, and deep within us we still trust our parents, jobs, businesses or relatives to provide, haven't we maimed God's ability to demonstrate the power of the impossible to us?

Indeed, the Bible indicates that human agents may deliver our answers: "Give, and it will be given to you. A good measure, pressed down, shaken together and running over, will be poured into your lap [by men]. For with the measure you use, it will be measured to you."[3]

However, this is a transactional, relative and conditional principle. And it does not indicate that God will specify which "men" God will use to make provisions possible. Our attitude should be to trust God for His arbitrary, unilateral choice of an agent or agents of our blessings. It is not for us to have a person in mind. What if that person doesn't deliver or dies, does it mean that God has failed us?

Not at all.

---

[3] Luke 6:38

Our trust should be in the invisible God who makes the invisible, visible, and the impossible, possible.

To do so, we ought to move from imaging to faithing. We ought to empty our heads of what we know about our world. We ought to act "unreasonably."

Well, I am a law professor and I understand what a dissonance this last statement sounds. But we are dealing with two dimensions here – the reasonable and the faithing. The reasonable belongs to the realm of the possible; the faithing to that of the impossible.

Therefore, in matters of law, I would use reason. But when dealing with the Spiritual God, I would use faith – going far beyond reason and delving in the impossible.

In fact, this reasoning is not farfetched. When beloved ones die, people are quick to say that they have gone to heaven. By heaven they mean that those beloveds are in another form, another realm. When Jesus, our Lord, was teaching on prayer, He told His disciples to address their prayers to the "Heavenly

Father."[4] The rendition "Our Father, who art in heaven," denotes that there are two dimensions, the earthly (reasonable) and the heavenly (spiritual). Those who pray to God, must approach Him from the higher realm of faith.

It is where our human reason, our thinking ends, where faith begins. When we pray for the impossible, we are engaging more than our human faculties, we are ditching them and, instead, choosing to believe in the "other" dimension. It is only then that we can call the impossible, possible. We can "see" things the way God sees them. We can anticipate their physical manifestation, just like God said, uttered the Word and the earth and all it contains manifested.[5]

Third, the power to go beyond imagination is already in us, "according to the power that worketh in us."

God does not ask us for what He has not already provided. He does not want us to second-guess Him or to deal with what could

---

[4] Matthew 6:9
[5] Genesis 1

be. That principle is established here: "For God is not unrighteous to forget your work and labor of love, which ye have shewed toward his name, in that ye have ministered to the saints, and do minister."[6]

God is not unfair, unjust.

God is fair.

The power to do the impossible already rests in us – all we need to do is to trust God and to use it. The results are God's. Ours is to do the fourth thing.

Fourth and last, give all the glory to God: "unto him be glory in the church by Christ Jesus throughout all ages, world without end. Amen."

When we pray for the impossible, our immediate attitude is to give thanks to God, even before we see the results: "Always give thanks to God the Father for everything in the name of our Lord Jesus Christ."[7]

---

[6] Hebrews 6:10
[7] Ephesians 5:20

And when the results manifest or become evident, we must give all the glory to God. Thanksgiving and ascription of glory to God, are the spiritual order of things, and they are unequivocal and universal:

> Sing to the Lord a new song;
> Sing to the Lord, all the earth.
> Sing to the Lord, bless His name;
> Proclaim good tidings of His salvation from
> day to day.
> Tell of His glory among the nations,
> His wonderful deeds among all the peoples.
> For great is the Lord and greatly to be praised;
> He is to be feared above all gods.
> For all the gods of the peoples are idols,
> But the Lord made the heavens.
> Splendor and majesty are before Him,
> Strength and beauty are in His sanctuary.
> Ascribe to the Lord, O families of the peoples,
> Ascribe to the Lord glory and strength.
> Ascribe to the Lord the glory of His name;
> Bring an offering and come into His courts.
> Worship the Lord in holy attire;
> Tremble before Him, all the earth.[8]

In conclusion, citizens of the earth, there is absolutely nothing impossible if you stand on faith and empty your doubtful human thinking. Don't depend on what you know, it will limit you. Rather, depend on what God knows and

---

[8] Psalm 96:1-9

trust Him. That's how the impossible becomes possible.

ABOUT THE AUTHOR

Charles Mwewa (LLB; BA Law; BA Ed; LLM) is a prolific author and researcher, poet, novelist, lawyer, law professor and Christian apologist. Mwewa has written no less than 40 books and counting in every genre and has exhibited his works at prestigious expos like the Ottawa International Book Expo and is the winner of the Coppa Awards for his signature publication, *Zambia: Struggles of My People*.

SELECTED BOOKS BY THIS AUTHOR

1. *ZAMBIA: Struggles of My People (First and Second Editions)*
2. *10 FINANCIAL & WEALTH ATTITUDES TO AVOID*
3. *10 STRATEGIES TO DEFEAT STRESS AND DEPRESSION: Creating an Internal Safeguard against Stress and Depression*
4. *100+ REASONS TO READ BOOKS*
5. *A CASE FOR AFRICA?S LIBERTY: The Synergistic Transformation of Africa and the West into First-World Partnerships*
6. *A PANDEMIC POETRY, COVID-19*
7. *ALLERGIC TO CORRUPTION: The Legacy of President Michael Sata of Zambia*
8. *BOOK ABOUT SOMETHING: On Ultimate Purpose*
9. *CAMPAIGN FOR AFRICA: A Provocative Crusade for the Economic and Humanitarian Decolonization of Africa*
10. *CHAMPIONS: Application of Common Sense and Biblical Motifs to Succeed in Both Worlds*
11. *CORONAVIRUS PRAYERS*
12. *HH IS THE RIGHT MAN FOR ZAMBIA: And Other Acclaimed Articles on Zambia and Africa*
13. *I BOW: 3500 Prayer Lines of Inspiration & Intercession from the Heart: Volume One*
14. *INTERUNIVERSALISM IN A NUTSHELL: For Iranian Refugee Claimants*
15. *LAW & GRACE: An Expository Study in the Rudiments of Sin and Truth*
16. *LAWS OF INFLUENCE: 7even Lessons in Transformational Leadership*

INDEX

J

Jesus Christ, 8
jobs, 5

L

Last Day, 3
law, 11
lawyer, 11

M

medical science, 3
mind, 3
minister, 8
money, 4, 5

O

Our Father. *See* heaven

P

parents, vii, 5
Paul. *See* Apostle Paul

prayers, 2
professor, 11

R

reasonable explanations, 5
reasoning, 5, 6
resurrection. *See* Last Day

S

saints, 8
Spiritual God, 6
Struggles of My People, 11, 13

T

thanksgiving, 8
the West, 13
think, 2
trust God, 5, 8

Z

Zambia, 11, 13, 14, 15

www.ingramcontent.com/pod-product-compliance
Lightning Source LLC
Chambersburg PA
CBHW061451050726
47593CB00004B/1544